Queens Park Rangers Quiz Book

101 Multiple Choice Questions
To Test Your Knowledge of QPR

Published by Glowworm Press
7 Nuffield Way
Abingdon OX14 1RL

By Chris Carpenter

Queens Park Rangers

This book contains one hundred and one informative and entertaining trivia questions with multiple choice answers. With 101 questions, some easy, some more challenging, this entertaining book will test your knowledge and memory of the club's long and successful history. You will be asked many wonderful questions on a wide range of topics associated with **Queens Park Rangers Football Club** for you to test yourself.

You will be quizzed on players, legends, managers, opponents, transfer deals, records, honours, fixtures, songs and much more. Educational, enjoyable and fun, The Queens Park Rangers Quiz book will provide the ultimate in entertainment for QPR fans of all ages.

2019/20 Season Edition

FOREWORD

When I was asked to write a foreword to this book I was deeply honoured.

I have known the author Chris Carpenter for many years and his knowledge of facts and figures is phenomenal.

His love for football and his talent for writing quiz books makes him the ideal man to pay homage to my great love Queens Park Rangers Football Club.

This book came about as a result of a challenge in a Lebanese restaurant of all places!

I do hope you enjoy the book.

Mike Phillips

Let's start with some relatively easy questions.

1. When were Queens Park Rangers founded?
    A. 1882
    B. 1884
    C. 1886

2. What is Queens Park Rangers' nickname?
    A. The Queens
    B. The Rangers
    C. The R's

3. Who has made the most appearances for Queens Park Rangers in total?
    A. Ian Gillard
    B. Clint Hill
    C. Tony Ingham

4. Who has made the most *League* appearances for the club?
    A. Kevin Gallen
    B. Ian Gillard
    C. Tony Ingham

5. Who is Queens Park Rangers' record goal scorer?
    A. Brian Bedford
    B. Kevin Gallen
    C. George Goddard

6. Who has scored the most penalties for the club?
    A. Les Ferdinand

B. Tony Ingham

C. Clive Wilson

7. Who is the fastest ever goal scorer for Queens Park Rangers?
   A. Les Ferdinand
   B. Tony Hazell
   C. Tommy Langley

8. Who started the 2019/20 season as manager?
   A. Ian Holloway
   B. Steve McClaren
   C. Mark Warburton

9. Who is the official club mascot?
   A. Jude the Cat
   B. Roland the Rat
   C. Spark the Tiger

10. Which of these is a well known pub near the ground?
   A. The Black Bull
   B. The Springbok
   C. The Wheatsheaf

OK, so here are the answers to the first ten questions. If you get eight or more right, you are doing very well so far, but don't get too cocky, as the questions do get harder.

A1. QPR were founded in 1886 after a merger between two clubs, St Jude's and Christchurch Rangers.

A2. Although their second official nickname is the Hoops, fans call their beloved club the R's which is basically an abbreviation of Rangers.

A3. Tony Ingham has made the most number of appearances for QPR making 548 appearances in total from 1950 to 1963. After hanging up his boots, he worked for the club in various roles including a spell as Commercial Manager. Legend.

A4. Tony Ingham made the most League appearances for the club, with 514 appearances in total. He never received a yellow card during his QPR career.

A5. Queens Park Rangers' record goal scorer is George Goddard, who played for the club between 1926 and 1934. He has 172 goals to his name.

A6. Clive Wilson scored 5 penalties for the R's in total.

A7. Tommy Langley scored the fastest goal in the history of QPR when he found the back of the net after just six seconds against Bolton Wanderers on 11th October 1980.

A8. Mark Warburton started the 2019/20 season as manager, having been appointed to the job in May 2019.

A9. QPR's mascot is Jude the Cat. He was named in honour of a moggy cat that lived inside the stadium many years ago. He recently replaced the last mascot Spark the Tiger.

A10. The Springbok Pub is the nearest pub to the ground and it's a pub covered in blue and white. Be prepared to queue for a pint though.

OK, let's have some questions about the ground.

11. Where do QPR play their home games?
    A. Loftus Road
    B. Rangers Stadium
    C. South Africa Road

12. What is the ground's current capacity?
    A. 17,934
    B. 18,439
    C. 19,394

13. What is the nearest tube station to the ground?
    A. Shepherd's Bush
    B. West Acton
    C. White City

14. What song do the players run out to?
    A. Glory Glory
    B. London Calling
    C. We are the Rangers Boys

15. What is the home end of QPR's ground known as?
    A. Loftus Road End
    B. Rangers End
    C. South Africa Road End

16. What is QPR's record attendance?
    A. 31,355
    B. 33,535
    C. 35,353

17. What is the name of the road on which QPR's ground is on?
    A. Australia Road
    B. New Zealand Road
    C. South Africa Road

18. Which stand has the biggest capacity?
    A. Ellerslie Road End
    B. South Africa Road Stand
    C. School End

19. What is the size of the pitch?
    A. 112 x 72 yards
    B. 114 x 72 yards
    C. 114 x 74 yards

20. When did the club get its artificial "plastic" pitch installed?
    A. 1981
    B. 1984
    C. 1988

Here are the answers to the last ten questions.

A11. QPR play their home games at Loftus Road, which has been their home since 1917.

A12. The total capacity of the ground is 18,439, all seated.

A13. White City station is the closest tube station to Loftus Road; it's only a five minute walk from the stadium.

A14. Queens Park Rangers run out to "London Calling" by The Clash.

A15. The home end of the ground is the Loftus Road End, often shortened to The Loft.

A16. The record home attendance 35,353 which was for a First Division match against Leeds United on 27th April 1974.

A17. The official postal address for QPR's stadium is South Africa Road, although one end of the ground is alongside Loftus Road.

A18. The South Africa Road stand has the biggest capacity among all four stands of the stadium. It is a two tier stand which includes the executive boxes, as well as the dugouts, changing rooms, offices, club shop and press conference rooms. The lower tier Paddocks contains the cheapest seats in the ground and the upper tier the most expensive seats.

A19. The pitch at Loftus Road is compact - it is 112 yards long by 72 yards wide. By way of comparison, the pitch at Wembley Stadium is 115 yards long by 75 yards wide.

A20. An artificial pitch of Omniturf was installed at Loftus Road in the summer of 1981; and it was the first such surface to be used in British professional football. It was removed in April 1998 because of football legislation, and was replaced with grass.

Here is a set of questions about the club's records.

21. What is Queens Park Rangers' record win in any competition?
    A. 11-0
    B. 12-0
    C. 13-0

22. Who holds the record for scoring the most number of goals in a single season for QPR?
    A. Brian Bedford
    B. George Goddard
    C. Rodney Marsh

23. What is the highest position the club has ever reached in the top division?
    A. 2nd
    B. 4th
    C. 6th

24. What is Queens Park Rangers' record win in the league?
    A. 8-1
    B. 9-2
    C. 10-3

25. Who did they beat?
    A. Tavistock
    B. Tranmere Rovers
    C. West Bromwich Albion

26. During which season?
    A. 1960/61
    B. 1970/71
    C. 1980/81

27. What is QPR's record defeat?
    A. 1-8
    B. 1-9
    C. 2-8

28. Who made the most appearances for the club as a goalkeeper?
    A. Paddy Kenny
    B. Phil Parkes
    C. David Seaman

29. Who has won the most international caps whilst a QPR player?
    A. Richard Dunne
    B. Alan McDonald
    C. Gino Padula

30. Who has scored the most hat tricks for Queens Park Rangers in the Premier League?
    A. Charlie Austin
    B. Les Ferdinand
    C. Bobby Zamora

Here are the answers to the last ten questions.

A21. QPR's record win is a 13-0 thrashing of non league side Tavistock during a pre-season friendly on 18 July 2011.

A22. English forward Rodney Marsh scored the most goals for the club in a single season, scoring 44 goals during the 1966/67 season.

A23. QPR finished second in the First Division in the 1975/76 season.

A24. Queens Park Rangers record league win is a 9-2 victory whilst in Division 3.

A25. The R's defeated Tranmere Rovers in their record league victory.

A26. They registered their record win in a Division 3 match on 3 December 1960 during the 1960/61 season.

A27. Manchester United handed QPR their worst ever league defeat, winning 8-1 in a Division One match on 19 March 1969, during the 1968/69 season.

A28. Phil Parkes holds the record here, turning out between the sticks for the club 406 times.

A29. Alan McDonald holds the record for the most number of international caps whilst being a QPR player, with 52 international caps to his name for Northern Ireland.

A30. Les Ferdinand holds the record for the most number of hat-tricks in the Premier League, with two for the club.

Here is a set of questions relating to the League Cup triumph.

31. When did QPR win the League Cup?
    A. 1967
    B. 1968
    C. 1969

32. Who did QPR beat in the League Cup final?
    A. Blackburn Rovers
    B. Swindon Town
    C. West Bromwich Albion

33. What was the score?
    A. 3-2
    B. 2-1
    C. 2-0

34. Who scored QPR's first goal in the League Cup Final?
    A. Mark Lazarus
    B. Rodney Marsh
    C. Roger Morgan

35. Who scored QPR's second goal in the League Cup Final?
    A. Mark Lazarus
    B. Rodney Marsh
    C. Roger Morgan

36. Who scored QPR's winning goal in the League Cup Final?
   A. Mark Lazarus
   B. Rodney Marsh
   C. Roger Morgan

37. Who was the captain who lifted the League Cup?
   A. Clint Hill
   B. Mike Keen
   C. Joey Barton

38. Who was the manager that day?
   A. Gordon Jago
   B. Dave Sexton
   C. Alec Stock

39. How many Englishmen started the match for QPR?
   A. 7
   B. 9
   C. 11

40. What was the colour of the kit that QPR played in on the day?
   A. All blue
   B. All white
   C. All yellow

Here are the answers to the League Cup set of questions.

A31. QPR won the League Cup on 4th March 1967.

A32. QPR defeated West Bromwich Albion in their maiden League Cup triumph.

A33. Queens Park Rangers won 3-2, coming from 0-2 behind.

A34. The first goal scorer that lovely sunny day was Roger Morgan in the 63rd minute

A35. Rodney Marsh equalised in the 75th minute.

A36. Mark Lazarus got the winner in the 81st minute.

A37. Mike Keen was the captain of the 1967 League Cup winning QPR side, lifting the trophy to over 97,000 people at Wembley Stadium.

A38. QPR's manager that season was Alec Stock.

A39. All eleven players who started the game were English, as was the substitute. How times have changed.

A40. QPR played in an all white kit on the day.

I hope you're having fun, and getting most of the answers right.

41. What is the record transfer fee paid for a player by Queens Park Rangers?
    A. £11.5 million
    B. £12 million
    C. £12.5 million

42. Who was the record transfer fee paid for?
    A. Joey Barton
    B. Steven Caulker
    C. Christopher Samba

43. What is the record transfer fee received for a player by QPR?
    A. £10 million
    B. £11 million
    C. £12 million

44. Who was the record transfer fee received for?
    A. Charlie Austin
    B. Loic Remy
    C. Christopher Samba

45. What is the fewest number of goals that QPR has conceded in a league season?
    A. 25
    B. 28
    C. 33

46. Which boxer became a World Champion at the stadium?
    A. Henry Cooper
    B. Lennox Lewis
    C. Barry McGuigan

47. What is the club's official website?
    A. qpr.co.uk
    B. queensparkrangers.co.uk
    C. qprfc.co.uk

48. What is the club's official twitter account?
    A. @QPR
    B. @QPROfficial
    C. @SuperHoops

49. Who is the youngest player ever to represent Queens Park Rangers?
    A. Charlie Austin
    B. Adel Taarabt
    C. Frank Sibley

50. Who is the oldest player to ever represent the club?
    A. Ray Wilkins
    B. Des Farrow
    C. Tony Roberts

Here are the answers to the last ten questions.

A41. The record transfer fee paid by Queens Park Rangers for a player is £12.5 million.

A42. QPR paid £12.5 million to sign Christopher Samba from Anzhi Makhachkala in January 2013.

A43. The record transfer fee received for a QPR player is £12 million.

A44. QPR sold Christopher Samba back to Anzhi Makhachkala for £12 million, just six months after buying him.

A45. QPR conceded just 28 goals during the 1971/72 season in the old Division Two.

A46. Barry McGuigan defeated Eusebio Pedroza to win the World Boxing Association featherweight championship at the stadium on 8th June 1985. He became the first Irishman to be a boxing world champion in 35 years.

A47. qpr.co.uk is the club's official website.

A48. @QPR is the official twitter account of the club. It tweets multiple times a day, and it deserves far more followers than it has.

A49. Frank Sibley is the youngest player to have played for QPR, making his debut at just 15 years and 275 days old in a League Cup tie away at Aldershot on 3rd September 1963.

A50. Ray Wilkins holds the record for being the oldest QPR player. He made his last appearance for the club at the ripe old age of 39 years and 352 days.

I hope you're learning some new facts about the Hoops.

51. Who is Queens Park Rangers' oldest ever goal scorer?
    A. Richard Langley
    B. Alfred Hitch
    C. Ray Wilkins

52. Who is Queens Park Rangers' longest serving manager of all time?
    A. James Howie
    B. Alec Stock
    C. Jack Taylor

53. Which Rugby Union side played at Loftus Road in the late 1990s?
    A. Harlequins
    B. London Irish
    C. Wasps

54. What is the name of Queens Park Rangers' match day programme?
    A. Match Day News
    B. Match Day Rangers
    C. Hoops

55. Which QPR manager has the highest win percentage of all time?
    A. Iain Dowie
    B. Harry Redknapp
    C. Jim Smith

56. Which of these is a Queens Park Rangers fanzine?
    A. Beat about the bush
    B. Kick Up the Rs
    C. Loft on the side

57. What symbol is on the crest of QPR?
    A. A Crown, a football and hoops.
    B. The Crown Jewels
    C. A jester dressed in blue and white

58. What is Queens Park Rangers' motto?
    A. Let us be judged by our acts
    B. Nil Satis Nisi Optimum
    C. Pride above all

59. Who are considered as QPR's main rivals?
    A. Arsenal
    B. Brentford
    C. Chelsea

60. What could be regarded as the Queens Park
    Rangers' most well-known song?
    A. Glory To The Rangers Boys
    B. Stand Up The Rangers Boys
    C. We Are The Rangers Boys

Here are the answers to the last ten questions.

A51. Ray Wilkins is the oldest ever goal scorer for Queen Park Rangers, and he was aged 36 years old and 338 days old when he scored in the home game against Liverpool on 18th August 1993.

A52. Alec Stock is the club's longest serving manager. He spent nine years at the helm from August 1959 to August 1968, and was in charge for 439 matches.

A53. Loftus Road was home to Wasps from September 1996 to the end of the 2001/02 season. It was all tied up in a deal which saw Chris Wright take control of both QPR and Wasps at the time.

A54. The name of Queens Park Rangers match day programme is "Hoops."

A55. Iain Dowie has the highest win percentage of any QPR manager ever with a win percentage of 53.3%. Mind you, he was only in charge for 15 games.

A56. Kick Up the R's is the most famous QPR fanzine.

A57. On the crest of Queens Park Rangers, there is a crown, a football and hoops.

A58. QPR have a very unique motto, which is "Let us be judged by our acts."

A59. Chelsea is considered to be the club's main rivals with the game known as the West London Derby.

A60. "We are the Rangers Boys" is arguably the most famous Queens Park Rangers song.

Let's give you some easier questions.

61. What is the traditional colour of QPR's home shirt?
    A. Blue and Green
    B. Blue and White
    C. Blue and Yellow

62. What is the traditional colour of QPR's away shirt?
    A. Green and Black
    B. Red and Black
    C. White and Black

63. Who is the current sponsor of Queens Park Rangers?
    A. Casino Royale
    B. Royal Jelly
    C. Royal Panda

64. Who was the club's first shirt sponsor?
    A. Guinness
    B. JD Sports
    C. KLM

65. Which of these airlines once sponsored QPR?
    A. Emirates
    B. Etihad
    C. Gulf Air

66. Who is the club's current chairman?
    A. Amit Bhatia
    B. Tony Fernandes

C. Lakshmi Mittal

67. Who was the club's first non-English signing?
    A. Don Givens
    B. Danny Maddix
    C. George Newlands

68. Who was QPR's first black player?
    A. Reg Allen
    B. Dexter Blackstock
    C. Leroy Rosenior

69. Who were QPR's first opponents in the Premier League?
    A. Arsenal
    B. Manchester City
    C. Manchester United

70. Who was QPR's leading goal scorer for the 2018/19 season?
    A. Luke Freeman
    B. Matt Smith
    C. Nahki Wells

Here are the answers to the last ten questions.

A61. The traditional colours of QPR's home shirt are blue and white hoops.

A62. QPR's away shirt is usually red and black, normally hoops.

A63. The current sponsor of the club is Royal Panda, an online casino company.

A64. Guinness were the first ever shirt sponsors of Queens Park Rangers, way back in 1983.

A65. Gulf Air sponsored Queens Park Rangers from 2008 to 2011. Other airlines that have sponsored the club include KLM, Air Asia and Malaysia Airlines.

A66. Amit Bhatia, an Indian businessman, is the current chairman of the club.

A67. Scottish full back George Newlands was the club's first non-English player.

A68. Leroy Rosenior was the first ever black player to put on a QPR shirt.

A69. Queens Park Rangers played their first Premier League game against Manchester City on August 17th 1992.

A70. Nahki Wells was the leading goal scorer for the 2018/19 season, with nine goals in total, including seven goals in the League.

71. What was the record transfer fee Queens Park Rangers paid for a British player?
    A. £6 million
    B. £7 million
    C. £8 million

72. Who was that fee paid for?
    A. Steven Caulker
    B. Rio Ferdinand
    C. Rob Green

73. In 2010, how much did QPR sell Raheem Sterling to Liverpool for?
    A. £600,000
    B. £700,000
    C. £800,000

74. What is the furthest stage QPR have reached in the FA Cup?
    A. Quarter Final
    B. Semi Final
    C. Final

75. Who is the current Chief Executive Officer?
    A. Mark Donnelly
    B. Les Ferdinand
    C. Lee Hoos

76. How many times have Australia played full internationals at Loftus Road?
    A. 2

B. 3

C. 4

77. What is Queens Park Rangers' training ground called?
    A. Empire Training Facility
    B. Harlington Sports Complex
    C. Imperial College Sports Ground

78. What is the highest number of goals that QPR has scored in a league season?
    A. 99
    B. 101
    C. 111

79. Which of these have never supplied kit to the club?
    A. Adidas
    B. Puma
    C. Umbro

80. Who was the first ever manager to manage Queens Park Rangers?
    A. James Cowan
    B. James Howie
    C. Ned Liddel

Here are the answers to the last ten questions.

A71. On 22 July 2014 QPR paid £8 million for a British defender.

A72. The transfer fee of £8 million was paid to Cardiff City for Steven Caulker.

A73. Raheem Sterling was sold to Liverpool for £600,000 but QPR secured a 20 per cent sell-on clause as part of the deal. So when he was transferred to Manchester City for £45 million in July 2015, QPR picked up a useful £9 million windfall.

A74. QPR have managed to reach the FA Cup final once, back in May 1982; losing 1-0 to Tottenham Hotspur in the replay, after the first match finished 1-1

A75. The current chief executive (CEO) at he club is Lee Hoos. He took up the role in May 2015.

A76. Australia has played three international matches at Loftus Road. They drew 1-1 with Ghana in 2006; lost 1-3 to Denmark in 2007 and drew 2-2 with South Africa in 2008.

A77. QPR's training ground is at the Imperial College Sports Ground, situated in Harlington, near Heathrow Airport.

A78. Queens Park Rangers scored 111 goals during the 1961/62 season, which is the highest number of goals scored in a season.

A79. Puma have never supplied kit to the club, whereas Adidas and Umbro, and many other manufacturers for that matter, have.

A80. James Cowan was the club's first manager, and he was in charge of 296 games from August 1906 to March 1913.

Here is the next set of questions.

81. Who was the last captain to lift a League trophy for QPR?
    A. Joey Barton
    B. Clint Hill
    C. Adel Taarabt

82. What shirt number does the mascot wear?
    A. 77
    B. 88
    C. 99

83. Where was Bright Osayi-Samuel born?
    A. Ghana
    B. Ivory Coast
    C. Nigeria

84. Who was placed alongside Rodney Marsh up front in the Club's Greatest XI?
    A. Brian Bedford
    B. Les Ferdinand
    C. George Goddard

85. During which season did Harry Redknapp take over as manager of the club?
    A. 2011/12
    B. 2012/13
    C. 2013/14

86. When was the last time QPR won a play-off final?

A. 2011/12
B. 2012/13
C. 2013/14

87. Who did they beat?
    A. Derby County
    B. Newport County
    C. Notts County

88. Who was the first ever kit sponsor for Queens Park Rangers?
    A. Adidas
    B. Admiral
    C. Umbro

89. What nationality is Jan Mlakar?
    A. Serbian
    B. Slovakian
    C. Slovenian

90. From which club did Adel Taarabt transfer?
    A. Benfica
    B. Marseille
    C. Tottenham Hotspur

Here are the answers to the last ten questions.

A81. Moroccan talisman Adel Taarabt was the last captain to lift a league trophy for QPR, the Championship trophy, at the end of the 2010/11 season.

A82. Jude the Cat, the official club mascot, wears shirt number 99.

A83. Osayi-Samuel was born in Okija in Nigeria.

A84. Les Ferdinand was put up front alongside Rodney Marsh in the club's greatest ever XI.

A85. Harry Redknapp took over the club in November 2012, so it was during the 2012/13 season.

A86. QPR won the 2013/14 Championship Play-Off Final.

A87. QPR beat Derby County 1-0 in the 2013/14 Play-Off Final to earn promotion back to the Premier League.

A88. QPR's first kit sponsor was Admiral, who started sponsoring the kit back in 1974.

A89. Promising forward Mlakar was born in Slovenia.

A90. After an initial successful loan period, Adel Taarabt joined QPR from Tottenham Hotspur for £1 million in August 2010.

Here is the final set of questions.

91. Who was the first English manager of Queens Park Rangers?
    A. Billey Birrell
    B. James Cowan
    C. Ned Liddell

92. Who was the first manager of QPR from outside the UK and Ireland?
    A. Luigi De Canio
    B. Mick Harford
    C. Paulo Sousa

93. Which manager led QPR back to the Premier League in 2011?
    A. Mark Hughes
    B. Harry Redknapp
    C. Neil Warnock

94. Which Manchester United legend joined QPR on a free transfer in the summer of 2014?
    A. Rio Ferdinand
    B. Darren Fletcher
    C. Nemanja Vidic

95. From which club did QPR sign goalkeeper Liam Kelly from?
    A. East Fife
    B. Livingston
    C. Rangers

96. Which Queens Park Rangers manager has the lowest win percentage?
    A. Gerry Francis
    B. Ray Harford
    C. Don Howe

97. How many honours did QPR win under Ian Holloway?
    A. 0
    B. 1
    C. 2

98. How many times have Queens Park Rangers won a League title (in all divisions)?
    A. 2
    B. 3
    C. 4

99. Who are the club's current kit manufacturers?
    A. Adidas
    B. Dryworld
    C. Errea

100.   Who owns the majority of shares in Queens Park Rangers?
    A. Tune Group
    B. The Mittal family
    C. Qatar Sports Investment Company

101. Who was voted as QPR's greatest ever manager?
   A. Ian Holloway
   B. Alec Stock
   C. Jack Taylor

Here are the answers to the last ten questions.

A91. Ned Liddel was the first English manager of the club, appointed back in 1924.

A92. Italian Luigi De Canio was the first ever manager of Queens Park Rangers to hail from a country other than the UK and Ireland.

A93. Neil Warnock successfully guided QPR to The Premier League, after winning the Football League Championship in 2011.

A94. Rio Ferdinand joined QPR for the 2014/15 season after he was released by Manchester United. He made only 12 appearances for QPR in his only season with the club.

A95. In June 2019, Kelly joined QPR from Scottish club Livingston.

A96. Under Ray Harford, QPR's win percentage is the lowest.

A97. Ian Holloway got the club promotion from Division Two at the end of the 2003/04 season, but he never won any silverware whilst at the club.

A98. Queens Park Rangers have won four league titles; they have won the Championship/Division Two twice and League 1 aka Division 3 twice.

A99. The current kit manufacturer is Errea, who took over from Dryworld in 2017.

A100. Tune Group of Malaysia owns 66 percent of the club's shares while Lakshmi Mittal owns 33 percent.

A101. Of course it was Alec Stock who was voted as the club's greatest ever manager.

That's it. I hope you enjoyed this book, and I hope you got most of the answers right. I also hope you learnt one or two new things about the club.

If you see anything wrong, or have a general comment, please visit the glowwormpress.com website.

Thanks for reading, and if you did enjoy the book, would you please leave a positive review on Amazon.

Printed in Poland
by Amazon Fulfillment
Poland Sp. z o.o., Wrocław

51560084R00026